DISCOVER DOGS WITH THE AMERICAN CANINE ASSOCIATION

I LIKE BORDER COLLIES!

Linda Bozzo

It is the mission of the American Canine Association (ACA) to provide registered dog owners with the educational support needed for raising, training, showing, and breeding the healthiest pets expected by responsible pet owners throughout the world. Through our activities and services, we encourage and support the dog world in order to promote best-known husbandry standards as well as to ensure that the voice and needs of our customers are quickly and properly addressed.

Our continued support, commitment, and direction are guided by our customers, including veterinary, legal, and legislative advisors. ACA aims to provide the most efficient, cooperative, and courteous service to our customers and strives to set the standard for education and problem solving for all who depend on our services.

For more information, please visit www.acacanines.com, email customerservice@acadogs.com, phone 1-800-651-8332, or write to the American Canine Association at PO Box 121107, Clermont, FL 34712.

Published in 2019 by Enslow Publishing, LLC.
101 W. 23rd Street, Suite 240, New York, NY 10011

Library of Congress Cataloging-in-Publication Data

Names: Bozzo, Linda, author.
Title: I like border collies! / Linda Bozzo.
Description: New York : Enslow Publishing, 2019. | Series: Discover dogs with the American Canine Association | Audience: K to Grade 3. | Includes bibliographical references and index.
Identifiers: LCCN 2018002880| ISBN 9781978501898 (library bound) | ISBN 9781978502567 (paperback) | ISBN 9781978502574 (6 pack)
Subjects: LCSH: Border collie—Juvenile literature.
Classification: LCC SF429.B64 B69 2019 | DDC 636.737/4—dc23
LC record available at https://lccn.loc.gov/2018002880

Printed in the United States of America

To Our Readers: We have done our best to make sure all websites in this book were active and appropriate when we went to press. However, the author and the publisher have no control over and assume no liability for the material available on those websites or on any websites they may link to. Any comments or suggestions can be sent by email to customerservice@enslow.com.

Photo Credits: Cover, p. 1 Erik Lam/Shutterstock.com; p. 3 (left), p. 13 (left) Dora Zett/Shutterstock.com; p. 3 (right) Bigandt.com/Shutterstock.com; pp. 5, 6 Aneta Jungerova/Shutterstock.com; p. 9 Dusan Zidar/Shutterstock.com; p. 10 Skorzewiak/Shutterstock.com; p 13 (right) graphicphoto/Thinkstock/(collar), Luisa Leal Photography/Shutterstock.com (bed), gvictoria/Shutterstock.com (brush), exopixel/Shutterstock.com (dishes), © iStockphoto.com/Lisa Thornberg (leash, toys); p. 14 Frank11/Shutterstock.com; p. 17 Beate Zoellner/F1online/Getty Images; p. 18 Tyler Olson/Shutterstock.com; p. 19 Puhach Andrei/Shutterstock.com; p. 21 Rob Byron/Shutterstock.com.

Enslow Publishing
101 W. 23rd Street
Suite 240
New York, NY 10011
USA
enslow.com

CONTENTS

IS A BORDER COLLIE RIGHT FOR YOU? 4

A DOG OR A PUPPY? 7

LOVING YOUR BORDER COLLIE 8

EXERCISE 11

FEEDING YOUR BORDER COLLIE 12

GROOMING 15

WHAT YOU SHOULD KNOW 16

A GOOD FRIEND 19

NOTE TO PARENTS 20

WORDS TO KNOW 22

READ ABOUT DOGS 23

INDEX 24

IS A BORDER COLLIE RIGHT FOR YOU?

Border collies need lots of outdoor space to run. If you live on a farm or on a large piece of land, a border collie might be a good choice for your family.

Don't expect a border collie to lay around the house!

A DOG OR A PUPPY?

Border collies are known as the smartest of all dog breeds. This makes them easy to train. If you do not have time to train a puppy, you may want an older border collie instead.

An experienced dog owner is best for border collies.

LOVING YOUR BORDER COLLIE

Love your border collie by giving him a job to do. He enjoys playing dog sports, such as catching Frisbees.

Border collies were bred in the hilly area between Scotland and England to herd sheep.

EXERCISE

Border collies are always ready for action. Long walks on a leash or games like fetch will help keep your border collie busy.

Border collies are medium-sized dogs.

FEEDING YOUR BORDER COLLIE

Border collies can be fed wet or dry dog food. Ask a veterinarian (vet), a doctor for animals, which food is best for your dog and how much to feed her.

Give your border collie fresh, clean water every day.

Remember to keep your dog's food and water dishes clean. Dirty dishes can make a dog sick.

Do not feed your dog people food. It can make her sick.

Your new dog will need:

a collar with a tag

a bed

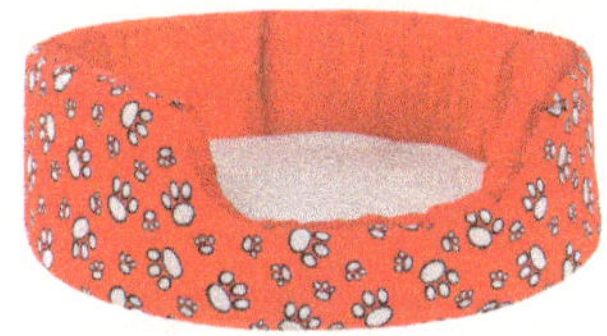

a brush

food and water dishes

a leash

toys

GROOMING

Border collies shed. This means their hair falls out. They need to be brushed often to remove dead hair. They can be bathed when needed. Make sure you use shampoo made specially for dogs.

Your border collie's nails will need to be clipped. A vet or groomer can show you how. Your dog's ears should be cleaned, and his teeth should be brushed by an adult.

WHAT YOU SHOULD KNOW

Border collies need to exercise their brains as much as their muscles.

Because they are herding dogs, border collies are not good with other small dogs or pets.

Border collies do best with an owner who is active and has lots of time to spend with them.

You will need to take your new dog to the vet for a checkup. He will need shots, called **vaccinations**, and yearly checkups to keep him healthy. If you think your dog may be sick or hurt, call your vet.

A GOOD FRIEND

Smart, loving, and fun, the border collie makes a good friend for many years.

A healthy border collie can live as long as 17 years.

NOTE TO PARENTS

It is important to consider having your dog spayed or neutered when the dog is young. Spaying and neutering are operations that prevent unwanted puppies and can help improve the overall health of your dog.

It is also a good idea to microchip your dog, in case he or she gets lost. A vet will implant a microchip under the skin containing an identification number that can be scanned at a vet's office or animal shelter. The microchip registry is contacted, and the company uses the ID number to look up your information from a database.

Some towns require licenses for dogs, so be sure to check with your town clerk.

For more information, speak with a vet.

There are many dogs, young and old, waiting to be adopted from animal shelters and rescue groups.

Words to Know

active Always keeping busy.

fetch To go after a toy and bring it back.

groomer A person who bathes and brushes dogs.

leash A chain or strap that attaches to the dog's collar.

shed When a dog's hair falls out so new hair can grow.

vaccinations Shots that dogs need to stay healthy.

veterinarian (vet) A doctor for animals.

Read About Dogs

Books

Clay, Kathryn. *Farm Dogs*. North Mankato, MN: Capstone Press, 2013.

Gagne, Tammy. *Collies, Corgies and Other Herding Dogs*. North Mankato, MN: Capstone Press, 2016.

Gray, Susan Heinrichs. *Border Collies*. New York, NY: AV2 by Weigl, 2017.

Websites

American Canine Association Inc., Kids Corner
www.acakids.com
Visit the official website of the American Canine Association.

National Geographic for Kids, Pet Central
kids.nationalgeographic.com/explore/pet-central
Learn more about dogs and other pets at the official site of the National Geographic Society for Kids.

INDEX

B
bathing, 15
bed, 13
brush, 13, 15
C
checkups, 18
collar, 13
D
dishes, 12, 13
E
ears, 15
England, 8
exercise, 11, 16
F
farm, 4
fetch, 11
food, 12
Frisbee, 8
G
grooming, 15
H
herding, 8, 16
L
land, 4
leash, 11
license, 20
lifespan, 19
M
microchip, 20
N
nails, 15
neutering, 20
O
older dog, 7
P
puppy, 7
R
running, 4
S
Scotland, 8
sheep, 8
shelter, 20
size, 11
spaying, 20
sports, 8
T
tag, 13
teeth, 15
toys, 13
training, 7
V
vaccinations, 18
vet, 12, 15, 18, 20
W
walks, 11
water, 12